# GIVE Thanks baby

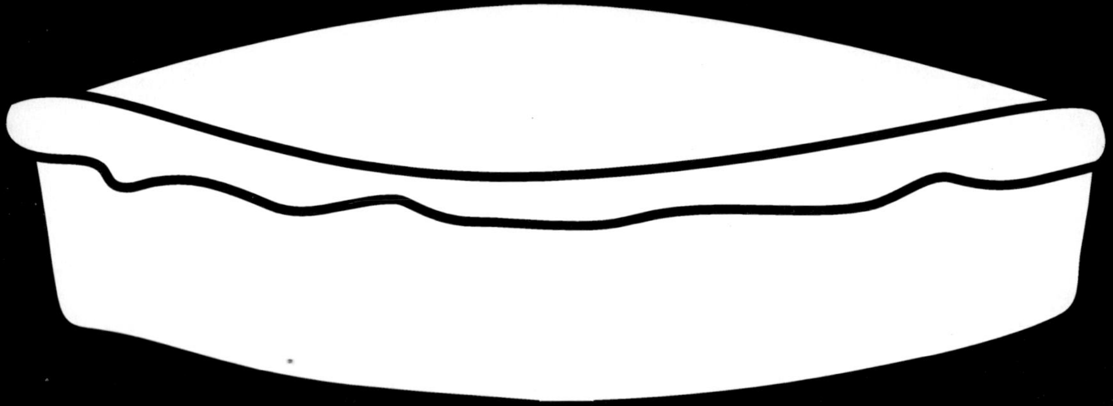

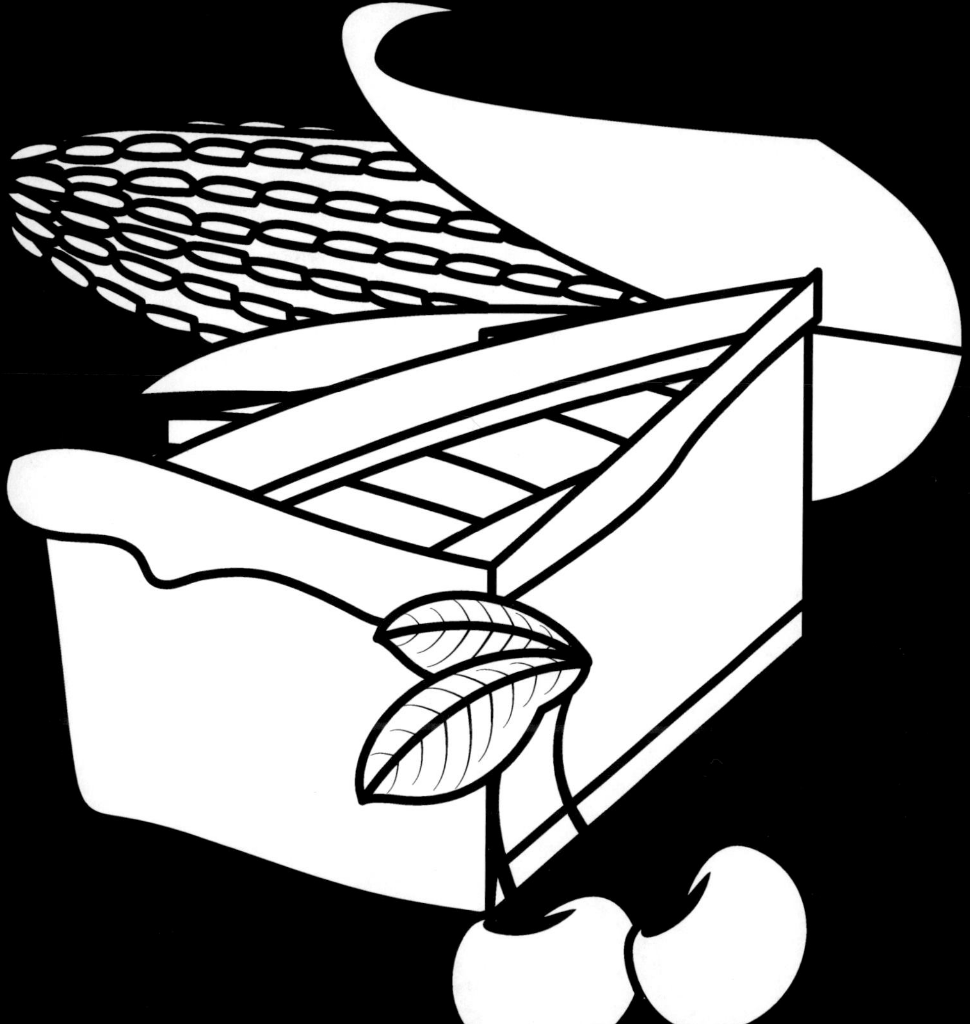

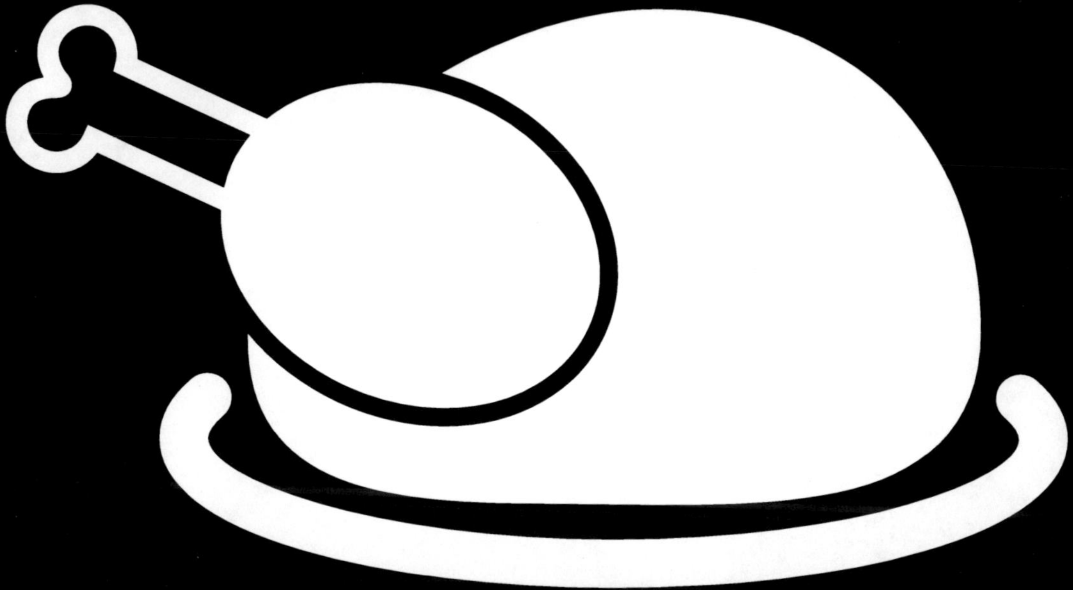

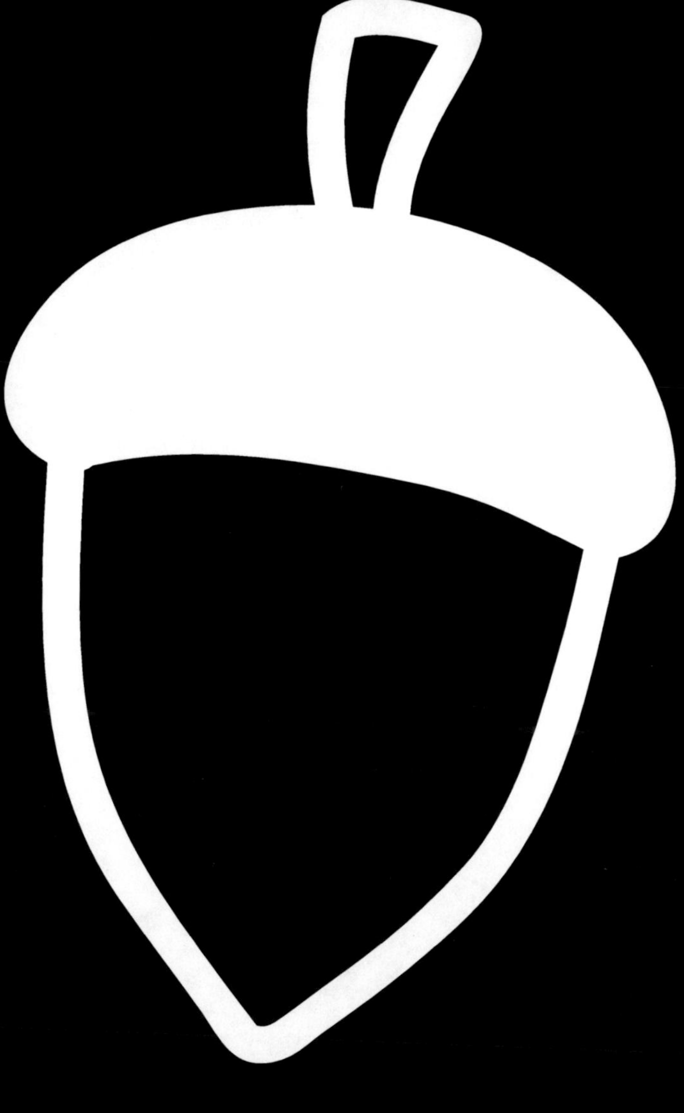

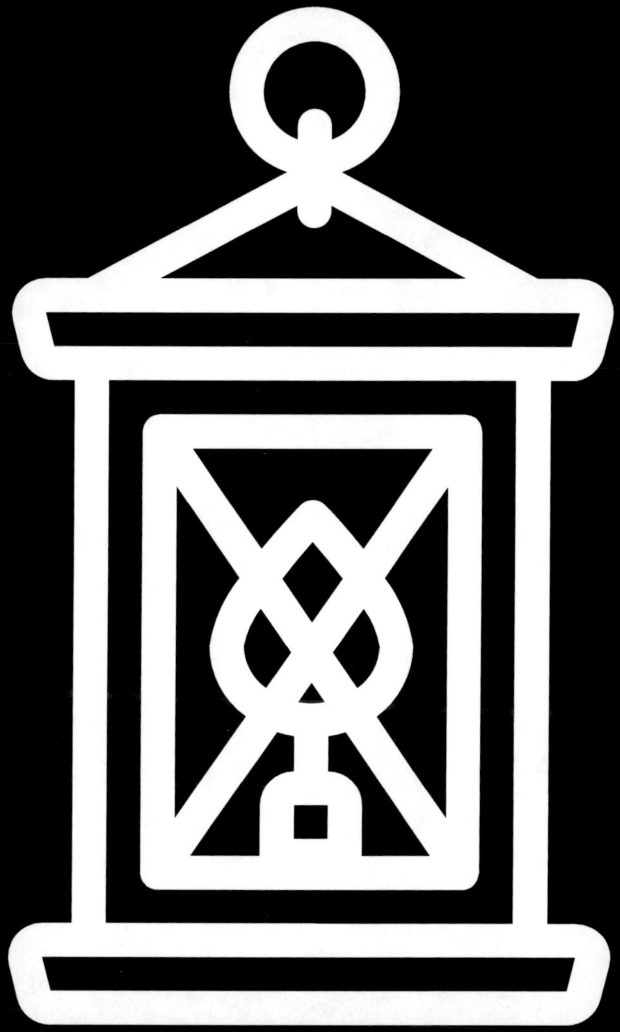

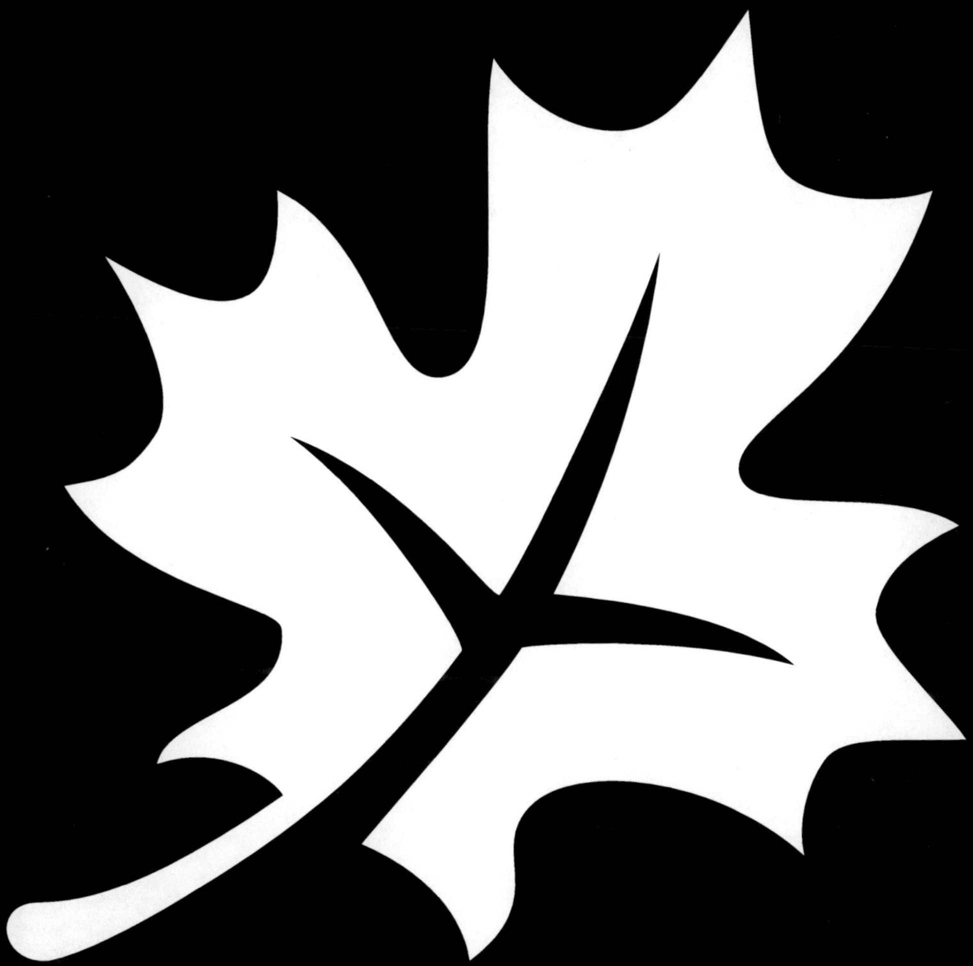

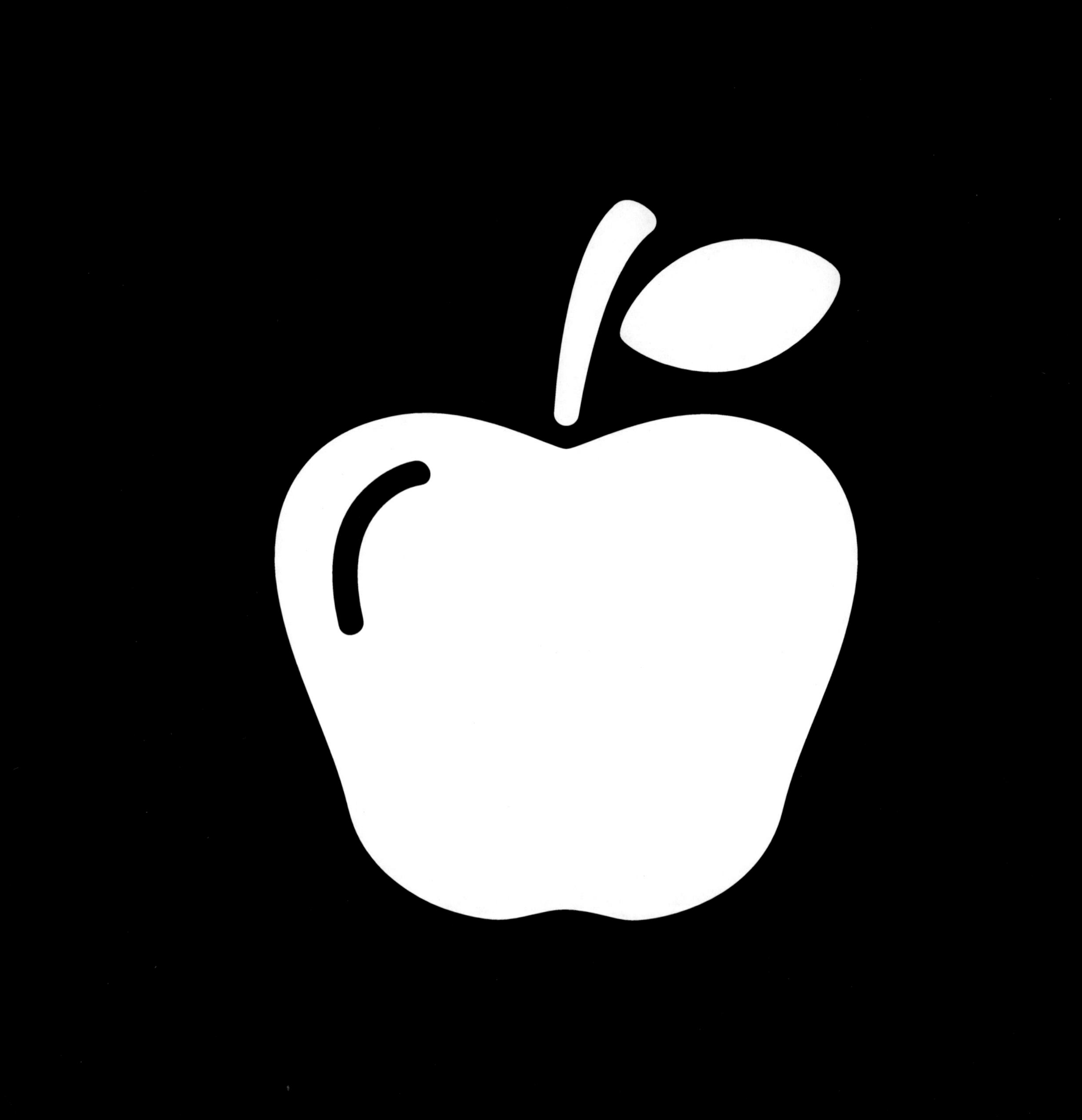

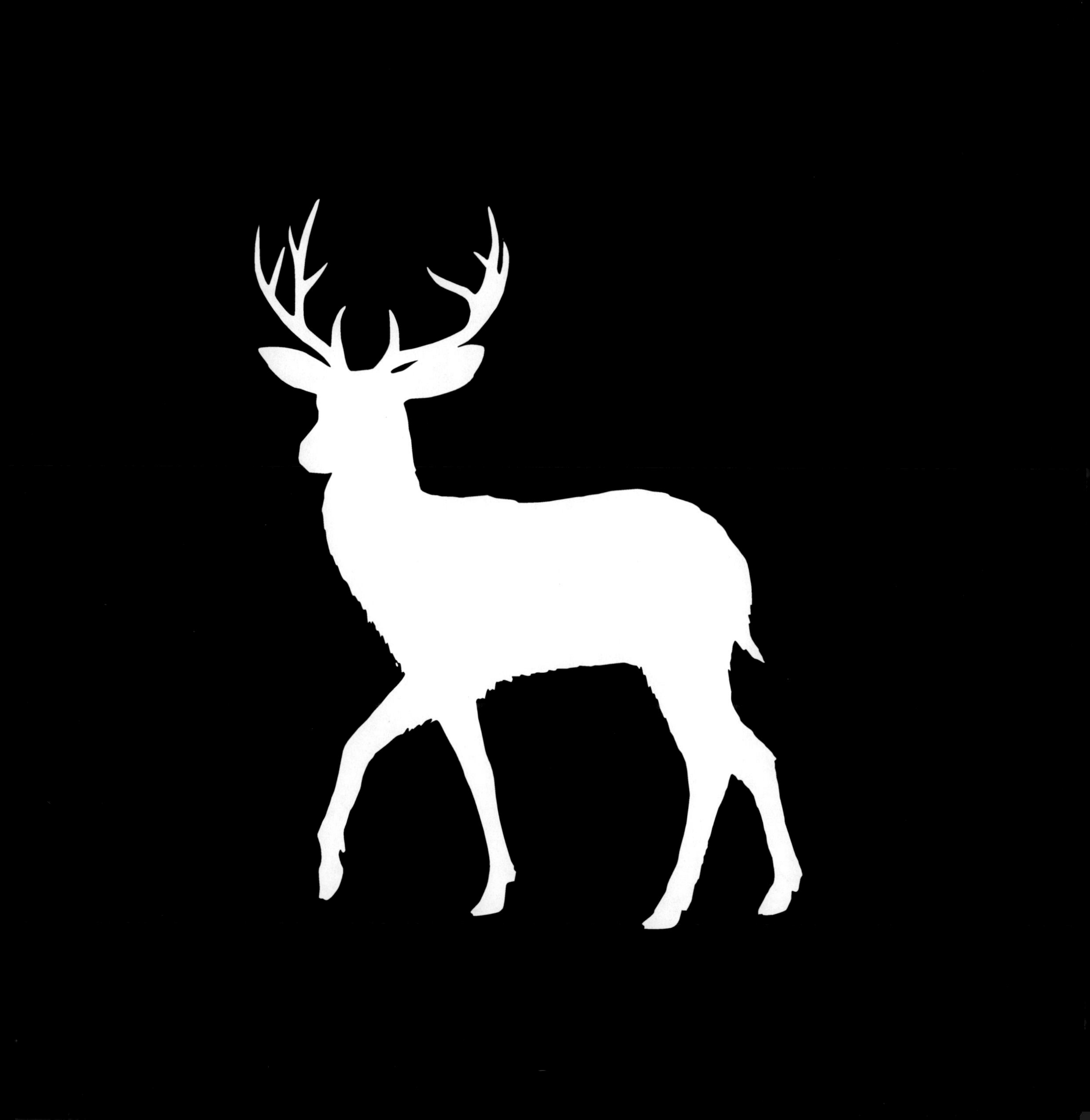

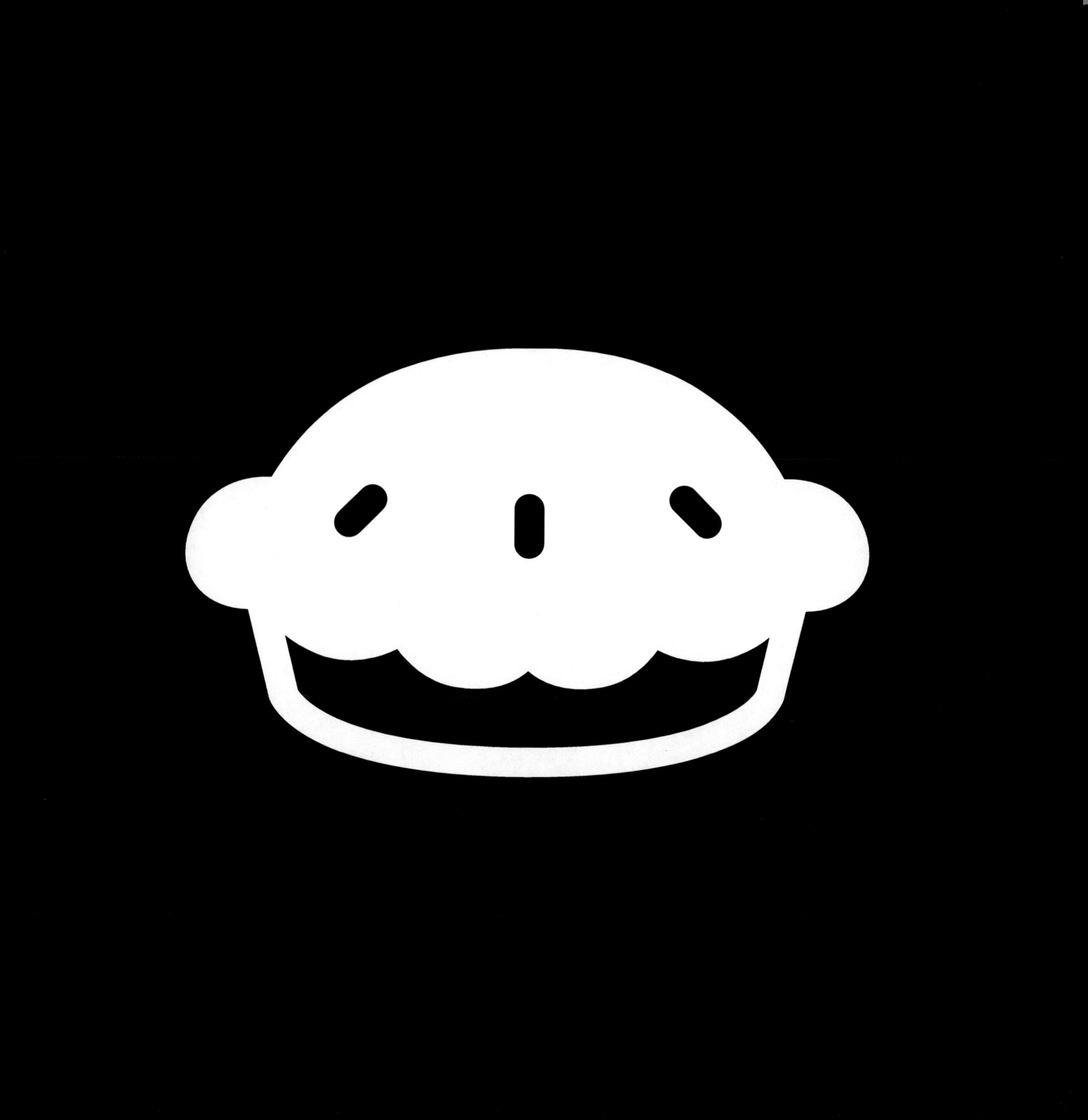